Cartoons
for
Thinking

Issues in Ethics
and Values

Second Edition
Revised, Expanded, and Updated

text by
Joseph P. Hester
Don R. Killian

cartoons by
Doug Marlette

Royal Fireworks Press
Unionville, New York
Toronto, Ontario

ABOUT THE AUTHORS

Doug Marlette's political cartoons have appeared in *Time, Newsweek, U.S. News and World Report, The Christian Century,* and *Rolling Stone.* He now has a feature cartoon, *Kudzu.* He has published five books of cartoons and his work is syndicated to 100 newspapers in the U.S. and abroad through King Features Syndicate. Marlette is a graduate of Florida State University, where he majored in Philosophy and minored in Art.

Don R. Killian is a graduate of Davidson College and Appalachian State University. He has done graduate work toward a Doctorate in Social Psychology at the University of Colorado, the University of North Carolina at Greensboro, and the University of Georgia. He is now Assistant for Recruitment and Professional Development at Gaston Community College, Gastonia, North Carolina.

Joseph P. Hester received a Doctorate in Philosophy from the University of Georgia in 1972. He is author of the book, *Philosophy For Young Thinkers,* and works as a gifted specialist and consultant for school systems throughout the nation. He has authored many articles in both philosophical and educational journals and is currently engaged in developing a K-12 gifted curriculum in the area of philosophical problem solving.

Originally published in 1988 by Trillium Press, Inc.

Royal Fireworks Press
First Avenue
Unionville, NY 10988
(914) 726-4444
FAX: (914) 726-3824

Royal Fireworks Press
78 Biddeford Avenue
Downsview, Ontario
M3H 1K4 Canada
FAX: (416) 633-3010

ISBN: 0-89824-007-7   Paperback

Printed on acid-free recycled paper by the Royal Fireworks Printing Co. of Unionville, New York.

TABLE OF CONTENTS

INTENDED USES OF THIS BOOK

This book can be used with students to develop the following skills:
1. Creative Problem Solving
2. Higher Level Reasoning/Thinking
3. Group Dynamics, including:
    a. Leadership
    b. Communication
    c. Conflict Resolution
    d. Team Building

The content of this book can be used in the following courses or subjects:
1. Debate/Communications
2. Sociology
3. History
4. Political Science
5. Social Issues/Problems
6. Creative Problem Solving
7. Human Relations/Attitudes
8. Group Dynamics
9. Philosophy/Ethics/Values
10. Religion
11. Minority Relations
12. Civics

SECTION ONE
THINKING ABOUT THINKING

Students should refer to this section of the book before and during all debates and discussions.

Planning for Thinking

This book is designed for the teacher and the student who desire to go further, dig deeper, and reason about the fundamental issues of contemporary living. The political/social cartoons stimulate reasoning and debate, and permit students to create their own cartoons and develop these into written research projects. This book is designed to allow students to discover uniquely creative outlets for their ideas.

Students may use these lessons individually or with a group. *The Mind Builders* activities are specifically designed to be used in small group situations. Small groups effectively promote discussion, leadership, and communication skills. Many ideas can be presented and evaluated. It will be the responsibility of the teacher to give guidance as their students begin the process of analysis and creative evaluation. Both teacher and student have the opportunity to turn these carefully designed activities and mind building exercises into products that will be useful for years to come.

The purposes of this book are:

1. To engage students in the process of re-thinking significant human problems

2. To provide students with practice in communications and other group dynamics skills

3. To assist students in developing their reasoning skills capacity

4. To help students develop team building and leadership skills

A Reasoning Skills Network

Before students utilize the following network of reasoning and problem-solving skills (skills 1-6), they should focus their attention upon the purpose of keeping an open mind to examining different points of view when attacking a major human problem.

Students should understand that "thinking," (and all that this word means) to be effective, is always directed at some purpose—to fill in a gap in information, to suggest an alternative solution, or to make the best decision one can possibly make in a given situation and under a particular set of circumstances.

Bruno Leone, in this series of books on *The Isms*, tells us why we should consider different points of view in our own decision-making. First, to determine the truth, a person should examine a wide variety of opinion. Wide reflection in creative problem solving and decision making is a must. Opinions that represent the middle of the road and those that represent extremes at either end will yield information valuable to our final solution, product, or decision.

Second, he tells us that to have a good grasp of our own viewpoint, we must first understand the point of view and the arguments of those with whom we disagree. It is a wise thing to be able to repeat back to a person correctly, the very argument or position which s/he has just given before rendering a reply to it. If we do not fully understand the point of view of our opponent, we will not fully grasp the significance of our own position. Listening and comprehending are a must in effective problem solving.

Finally, Leone tells us that we should avoid considering our own position as being common sense and the most rational position and the point of view of others as being, by definition incorrect. This will lead only to close-mindedness to the opinions of others. It will block any future explorations and evaluations. Listening to others will more effectively facilitate the solving of problems than closing one's mind to those who may differ with you.

Skill 1: Problem Identification

Perhaps the most essential skill in successful problem solving is the careful identification of the problem to be solved. Basic *issues* should be stated. Any *conclusions* reached must be identified. *Assumptions* and *reasons* that support the conclusion should be located, and the stated or unstated *implications* of the conclusion clearly developed. Once this initial process has been completed, the student is ready for further analysis and assessment.

Skill 2: Process/Strategy Selection

How does the student begin the process of creative problem solving? Students do not always know where to start; yet they can enhance the final product of their research if they first clearly define a method of approach. For example, effective process selection will include:

a.   Identifying the problem to be studied

b.   Identifying the relevant sources of information

c.   Evaluating the credibility of these sources

d.   Being able to pull appropriate information from these sources

e.   Applying this information to the problem

f.   Combining new ideas and information to create new and interesting solutions

Skill 3: Organizing and Presenting Information

In most tasks that require intelligent performance, the student must organize and present information in a comprehensible, useful manner. The presentation of information in written form, in graphs, charts, tables and maps will enhance the communication process. Also, the student must learn the important skill of oral presentation.

Skill 4: Solution Monitoring

Students need a method for keeping track of the steps in the problem-solving process. They also need to keep up with the information that they have collected as they moved through the process of discovery. *Recording* what they have done, what they are *now doing*, and what *remains to be done*, is essential to successful solution finding. In this way, the student can determine if each step in the process has impacted sufficiently on the problem as a whole, in order to bring about a more suitable solution.

Skill 5: Feedback Sensitivity

The student must be sensitive to both internal and external feedback. Internal feedback comes from one's own understanding of how well task performance is going. External feedback comes from other people's perception of how

3

well the group as a whole is doing. Our sensitivity to feedback is a major determinant of our potential to improve; but sensitivity to feedback without the ability to translate it into a plan of action is unproductive. The student needs to learn how feedback can be used to change his/her performance.

Likewise, the teacher must master the skills of human relations in order to monitor and stimulate student learning.

Skill 6: Implementation of Action Plan

The skill of implementing a plan is both motivational and cognitive. Some students will be able to act effectively on what they know, some will not. Yet, it is this skill that demonstrates the difference between inadequate student performance and performance that reflects a high level of learning. The teacher should take time to help students develop and put into effect their plans of action.

Barriers to Effective Problem Solving

1. Lack of clarity and precision in stating the problem or the task to be considered.

2. Not getting the required information. The solution will be of low quality when information is inadequate.

3. Ineffective communication. Openly shared dialogue is important in team problem solving and is essential in communicating the results to others.

4. A competitive, critical atmosphere. Cooperation and trust are the important qualities to be nurtured in the group.

5. Groupthink and pressures toward conformity or toward a quick solution.

6. Poor motivation. The benefits of group participation must be stressed because students are often the best motivators of other students.

EXERCISE:
MANIPULATING HUMAN BIRTH

In March, 1987, the Vatican issued a controversial document calling for legal restraints on the medical manipulation of human birth, including invitro fertilization, surrogate motherhood, and the termination of flawed fetuses. Moral traditionalists of all faiths agreed that biomedical science must not be allowed to intrude on natural life processes.

On the other side of this issue some claimed that "...the church is a little out of touch with reality." With this claim, serious debate began on the issue, but the two sides have not grown closer to a consensus on the profound and important moral issues which pervade the problem.

If you wish to become involved in debating this issue with others, then you must first focus on understanding the issues involved and the ethical or moral alternatives open to those who are sensitive to the ethical nature of human life. This means that each debater must carefully and accurately identify the problem involved, any related subproblems and/or issues, and make an effort to understand how each side in the controversy perceives the problem. As the debate unfolds, you must strive for consistency in your solution-making. This also means that both the short and long range consequences of the positions under examination will need evaluation and validation. Any final solutions should also be assessed by a common moral criteria which should also be given wide and considered examination.

Once these steps have been undertaken, you will be able to come to terms with your own position on this matter, better understand the position(s) of those who differ with you, and stand a better chance to reach common ground with them.

The following suggestions may help you with your own problem solving:

1.   Research the problem carefully and try to state it in a single sentence.

2.   Identify and evaluate relevant sources of information and choose the most accurate and reliable sources on the subject to support your position.

3.   Next, you should pull from these sources the appropriate information and carefully separate it from mere opinion and belief.

4.   Questions of value need to be isolated. Words, such as "ought," "should," "good" or "bad," and "right from wrong," signify value statements. These statements will often be reflective of one's biases

5

and/or cultural background and, therefore, should be supported by careful reasoning.

5. Next, the information gained in your research should be applied to the problem in a logically consistent fashion. The combination of old and new ideas will many times create new and interesting solutions.

6. Finally, you should organize and present your own point of view, listen to the opinions of others, the criticisms of others, and be willing to revise your own position where necessary.

When debating the biomedical problem above, careful consideration needs to be given to the following questions:

a. To whom does a child of surrogate birth really belong?

b. Should a malformed fetus live or die?

c. Who should make these decisions?

d. Does ultimate moral authority lie with the church? the state? the individual? or some other person or group?

The effectiveness of your creative problem solving and decision making will be greatly improved when you are able to follow the steps outlined above. Patience and "cool" reflective thought are key elements in this process. Solutions, products, and decisions are always improved when subjected to the insights of others and the wisdom of reasoning and understanding.

Planning for Classroom Discussion

The basic teaching methodologies used in this text are group discussion and experimental learning conducted through a "team" or "varsity" approach. We use the group discussion method because we believe that the development of group skills is necessary for effective learning and for effective functioning in our society. We emphasize experiential learning because we believe students learn more when they are personally involved in the learning process. The reasoning and thinking skills we hope to improve in the students can best be developed utilizing these two methodologies through a team approach.

Both students and teachers should see the classroom as a place where they are learning and sharing their knowledge, their experience, and their insights. The classroom is not a one-way street where the teacher is an active participant and the student is a passive receiver of information; most of which is not retained in a way that benefits the student. Learning and sharing represent a dialogue, not a monologue. Teachers should listen to comments, experiences, feelings, and questions of their students. Thus, the teacher and student explore together, both learners, both getting new and deeper insights from their explorations.

Why are groups important? In essence, we become human through our functioning in groups. Most of our time is spent associating with people in groups. The way we see the world—and in fact, the way we see ourselves—is the direct result of our experiences in groups. Our basic physical, emotional, social, and spiritual needs are almost exclusively met in groups. It is not our nature to live alone: from infancy to old age we need to belong to groups.

In many ways, the groups to which we belong are the best "friends" we will ever have. The skills that enable us to function effectively in groups are among the most important we ever learn. This stresses the development of thinking, problem solving, group dynamic skills. Both students and teachers become involved in skill-building exercises and problem solving techniques.

Many people have difficulty working in groups because they do not know how to work well with others. We spend a great deal of time in groups, but many of our interactions are flawed. This book will help improve these interaction skills that we all need in our association with others.

There are at least two reasons which inhibit the development of effective group skills. First, our participation in the family group rarely encourages shared participation, particularly on an equal basis. Children, for the most part, grow up being told things by their parents, rarely sharing experiences with them. The basic group dynamic in the family is one of obedience to authority and deference to the status of parents. Second, the school usually does not encourage shared and cooperative efforts on the part of students and teachers. Students compete for grades, for the favor of the teacher, for a part in the school play, or for academic honors. We live in a society that stresses individualism, competition, dominance, and survival. Consequently, we tend to view others competitively and somewhat suspiciously—even when the situation does not warrant such a perception.

The group discussion and exercises in this book will attempt to create a teamwork atmosphere in the classroom by stimulating learning through shared ideas and cooperative efforts. We term the approach emphasized in this book as the "team" or "varsity" approach. That is, the class is so structured in terms of tasks and relationships that the entire team is working toward some common goals with the teacher acting as a kind of coach. The effectiveness of a classroom is greatly influenced by the quality of cooperation among the students and the teacher. Team building skills are incorporated into the exercises and mind builders in this book.

The main reason for the emphasis on team building is that increasingly our society is demanding that people solve many of their critical life problems through cooperative efforts with others. As stated earlier, most Americans receive little training in "teamwork" except from some sports participation as children. Effective teamwork involves an atmosphere of cooperation and mutual respect.

What is a team? First, the team produces results collectively that are superior to what could be achieved by those same individuals working independently. Secondly, team members have a stake in the output of their team. This means they are willing to work constructively to clear away barriers standing in their way.

The team or varsity approach to teaching has several benefits for the classroom.

— more resources can be brought into the learning process by virtue of all team members making a contribution.

— the team helps fulfill the members' need for recognition and achievement since all can make a contribution to the team effort.

— students learn a variety of behaviors, roles, and perspectives by working on different projects with a number of classmates.

— it is with groups that attitudes and values are learned; respect and appreciation of the views of others are reinforced in team efforts.

— team skills built in the classroom are transferable to other areas of the student's life; these skills may aid in adjusting to changes in the student's life, i.e., college, career, marriage, etc.

— teams stimulate and encourage creativity as ideas tend to be contagious— one idea in a group may trigger several others.

There are several problem behaviors that the teacher needs to look out for in classroom teams. Most of these problems can be remedied by building openness, trust, and respect for others into the team structure.

Problem Behaviors in Teams
— Non-participating behavior
— Monopolistic behavior
— Advice giving
— Hostile behavior
— Acting superior
— Criticizing others
— Personality conflicts

A Note on Leadership

Leadership involves a number of skills that can be acquired. Being able to recognize the skills, being able to determine what skill is needed, and being able to use it, is what team leadership is all about. Everyone is a potential leader and possesses certain leadership qualities. The team leader has the ability to bring these skills out in others. There are two basic skill clusters. One cluster of skills is associated with the task the team has been assigned. The other cluster is associated with helping team members work together better. Both sets of skills are essential if the team is to exhibit a high level of teamwork.

Notes on Using Teams As A Teaching Methodology

A good rule of thumb in any classroom is: the less the teacher talks, the more students learn. The team approach allows all students to participate actively in the learning process. Not only is learning facilitated by teamwork, but creativity as well. It is a common saying among behavioral scientists that there is no such thing as a creative person, only creative groups.

There are seven steps the teacher can take to increase motivation and morale in classroom teams. First, the team should be identified in some way either by a name or symbol. Second, the teacher should help teams build a tradition or history of accomplishments. Students can feel good about what they have achieved and this can be an incentive for future efforts. Third, at every opportunity the teacher should stress teamwork—reinforce teamwork behavior at every opportunity. Fourth, team members should recognize and praise contributions of teammates. Fifth, the team should have clear, attainable goals. Sixth, the teacher should reward the team when tasks are satisfactorily completed. Seventh, the teacher should encourage and tolerate disagreements.

In working through the units and exercises in this book, the teacher should remember the following points:

9

— students forget more than they learn

— best learning involves experience and practice

— students love to ask questions

— learning is related to change

— learning can be fun

— students need opportunity to practice

— learning involves stress

— students want to know why they are learning something

— students decide what they will learn

— most material is not learned the first time through

Strategies for Learning

As we study fundamental human issues, we must confront questions which elicit responses that require thought and analysis. As we become more accustomed to discussing fundamental human issues in a rigorously philosophical manner, we will be able to answer higher level questions with ease and flexibility.

During the questioning/discussion process we should make every effort to be interested, inquiring, and curious. The issues being discussed should relate to our own experiences and feelings. Although beginning on a personal level, discussion should move to a wider perspective, a perspective involving groups and/or nations of people.

The following questions serve as a guide to help teachers and students avoid the manipulation of a discussion in order to foster or practice one's own personal point of view. These questions can be applied generally to any problem area.

Questions to Promote Reasoning Skills

1. Literal Questions

Who or what was involved?
What happened?
What are the important details?
Is the point you are making that . . .?
Can I summarize your point as. . .?

2. Interpretive Questions

Why did it happen?
What does it mean?
What significance is it to others?
What are your reasons for saying that?
Are you not assuming something?
How do you explain your point of view?
How do you know that?
Does what you say presuppose something?
Is what you mean to say that. . .?
What do you mean when you use that word?

3. Evaluative Questions

Was it good? Why?
Did you like it? Why?
How was it valuable?
What standards did you use to explain its worth?
What other ways can you state that?
How else can we view this issue?

4. Creative Questions

What is going to happen next?
How do you feel about it?
How can you put this idea into practice?
What conclusions can you make?
Is it possible that. . .?
Are there other ways of looking at. . .?

Fallacies of Reason

Irving M. Copi, in his *Introduction to Logic*, identifies a fallacy as a type of incorrect argument; that is, a fallacy is a type of argument that may seem correct (it even may be an argument which we are psychologically persuaded to believe) but which proves, upon examination, not to be so. Copi divides the fallacies of reasoning into two broad categories: formal fallacies and informal fallacies.

Formal fallacies are certain patterns of mathematical reasoning related to patterns of valid inference to which they bear a superficial resemblance. To satisfy the purposes of this book, we shall be concerned only with informal fallacies, errors in reasoning which come about because of carelessness and inattention to our subject matter or through being misled by some ambiguity in the language used to formulate our argument. From Aristotle to the present day, various lists of these fallacies have appeared which put the number from thirteen to one hundred twelve.

For our purposes, we shall contend that there are only two basic informal fallacies, but that these two can appear in many different forms. These are...

1.   Fallacies of Relevance
     and
2.   Fallacies of Ambiguity.

Fallacies of relevance occur in situations where the facts and/or premise of an argument are irrelevant to the conclusion and therefore incapable of establishing the truth of the conclusion or solution to an argument. A number of particular types of irrelevant argument have been identified for our study:

1.   The appeal to force to cause acceptance of a conclusion or solution.

2.   Abusive language toward those who disagree with you (sometimes called the "genetic fallacy") for obvious reasons.

3.   Circumstantial arguments where what is believed to be true or false is believed because of who the person is that is doing the arguing.

4.   Argument from ignorance, which is to assume that something is true because no one has proven it false or that it is false because no one has proven it true.

5.   The appeal to authority is very common and akin to the circumstantial argument. This fallacy begins when we appeal to who or what a person is rather than to the facts of the case when arguing.

6.   Hasty generalization is the failure to recognize atypical cases and to classify all similar things, events, and people as alike in every way.

7.   Begging the question is another common fallacy which occurs when attempting to establish the truth of a proposition, we assume true the very thing that we are trying to prove.

13

Fallacies or ambiguity or clearness occur in arguments whose formulations contain ambiguous words or phrases, whose meanings shift and change more or less subtly in the course of the argument and thus render it fallacious. We should be clear when using words with more than one meaning, and make sure that when writing a report, our grammar is clear and correct. Clearness of speech and in the written word and saying what you mean are ways of avoiding these fallacies.

DILEMMA DEBATE #1:
THINKING INDEPENDENTLY

How important is independent and critical thinking? Each day gives us many opportunities to develop our thoughts. Our brains can take in, process, and use 600 memories per second; that is, 36,000 memories per minute; 2,160,000 per hour and over 51,000,000 memories per day.

An untapped reservoir of ideas, facts, opinions, beliefs, theories, and experiences lies between our ears. To use the brain effectively, thinking should be directed toward solving important problems. Thinking should be purposeful.

Critical thinking will help you disseminate facts, make comparisons, discover assumptions, identify implications, and evaluate solutions. It will involve analyzing data, ordering and interpreting information, and selecting relevant facts for application.

Use critical thinking skills as you interpret the political cartoons on the following page.

Discussion

1. Carefully study the cartoon. Observe the words and actions of the sheep.

2. Is what the sheep are saying consistent or inconsistent with what they are doing?

3. Can you name real-life situations which are or have been similar to what is happening in the cartoon? Write them down and report them to the class or your group.

4. Choose one answer that a sheep is giving to ''life's problems.'' Do you agree or disagree with the sheep? How did you reach your conclusion.

5. Below are listed some barriers to clear and independent thinking. What does each of the barriers mean? Develop some examples of each through class or group discussion.

    a) Impulsiveness   d) Inability to Concentrate
    b) Missing the Meaning   e) Dogmatic Behavior
    c) Rigidity of Thinking   f) Resistance to New Ideas

15

16

Mind Builder
People Are Like . . .

1. Form the class into groups of five.

2. Ask the group members to share their real-life situations with each other. Group members now compare their real-life situations to see if there are any similarities. Students discuss reasons for the similarities and differences.

3. Each group writes on the chalkboard two real-life situations they have in common.

4. Conduct a hands-up poll to see how many students have experienced each of the items listed on the board.

5. In groups of five or six discuss and list as many similarities between human beings and sheep as you can. Then list the similarities. . .
   a. between human beings and bees;
   b. between human beings and ants;
   c. between human beings and monkeys;
   d. between human beings and any other animals the class would like to discuss.

DILEMMA DEBATE #2:
THE DESCENT OF MAN

The political/social cartoon in this dilemma appeared in *The Charlotte Observer* on April 8, 1980. The purpose of a political or social cartoon is to express a point of view. When the particular point of view of the cartoon is recognized by the reader, it can be a thought-provoking experience. It can add meaning and significance to the reader's life.

Discussion

1. What viewpoint is being expressed by this cartoon?

2. This activity is entitled, "The Descent of Man." Do you think the cartoon should be entitled, "The Ascent of Man?" Give reasons for your opinion.

3. What reasons do you think the author had for creating this cartoon?

4. Do you think the viewpoint in this cartoon focuses on a vital problem? What is this problem?

5. Do you see any hidden messages in the symbolism of this cartoon? What are they?

Mind Builder
Communicating Viewpoints

1. By a show of hands, students display their agreement or disagreement with the interpretation of the cartoon.

2. The class forms dyads (two person groups) — one member agreeing with the point of view of the cartoon and the other disagreeing.

3. Each student states his reasons for agreeing or disagreeing with his partner. After each has stated his view, the other member relates as clearly and accurately as possible the viewpoint different from his own. This must be done to the satisfaction of his partner.

4. In groups of four, two agreeing and two disagreeing, discuss and list the reasons the author might have had for creating this cartoon. Share your ideas with other groups in the class.

SECTION TWO
LIVING TOGETHER

Living together implies a sense of community among a group of people. The word "community" is an amazingly rich word, full of history and loaded with meaning. It comes from the Latin word "communis," which means "in common" or "sharing." Accordingly, a community consists of people living closely together, sharing meaning, similar feelings, attitudes, values, and goals. Communities can be large or small—a city, neighborhood, family, or group. Often these similarities are based on national, ethnic, political, or geographic origins.

Although ideal communities are made up of people living close to one another, sharing a common culture, a set of common values, helping each other when needed while leading independent lives—communities sometimes fail.

When communities fail, one effect may be a feeling of alienation among its members. "Alienation" refers to the feeling of not being involved in one's group or community. It is a feeling of being alone and apart from those who live around you. It is also a feeling of powerlessness and can result in a drastic lowering of a person's expectations for himself.

The cartoons and discussions on the following pages are concerned with community failures. They deal with human dignity, equality, discrimination, and military aggression. Hopefully, they will involve you in discussing the concept of human rights, the very foundation of the community process.

Mind Builder
Community Interdependence

The purpose of this exercise is to demonstrate the interdependence of people living in a community.

There are four kinds of problems each of us faces in relation to others in a community. Our satisfactions in life depend on the extent to which we are able to solve these problems.

Everyone needs to: **obtain** some things from others (i.e., food), **retain** some things from others (i.e., property), **contain** some things in others (i.e., disease), and **dispose** some things to others (i.e., labor).

1.   Divide the class into groups of four students. Assign one of the above four problems to each student in the group.

2.   Each student writes out a definition of his problem in terms of how it relates to other people in the community. Each student shares his definition with other members of his group.

3.   Have each group discuss and make a list of things obtained from others, retained from others, contained in others, and disposed in others.

4.   Discuss why some people have difficulty meeting these needs.

5.   Discuss how the following factors influence one's ability to meet these needs.
     a.   Economic Factors   d.   Sex
     b.   Occupation   e.   Religion
     c.   Race   f.   Ethnic Background

6.   Are there any people in your community who continually fail to meet these needs? If so, why? Are these people separated in some way from the rest of the community? Discuss.

7.   Have a class discussion about some possible solutions to feelings of separateness and alienation.

DILEMMA DEBATE #3:
OUR NATION'S POOR

In the United States, we supposedly govern ourselves according to the democratic principles of equality and non-discrimination. These principles are the basis of the myth that the United States is a classless society. In short, many believe that because all men are "created" equal, they are equal in all ways—that they have equal opportunity to acquire wealth, privilege, and power. But the tremendous gaps between the haves and the havenots grow wider each decade in America. In a society, those who remain at the bottom of the socio-economic system are called "minorities" and are subjected to discriminatory practices by the wider society.

Minorities are victims of prejudice, discrimination, and unequal opportunities in the economic system. They are generally poor, are ill-fed and clothed, and live in substandard housing. Thus, their life-chances in all areas of life have been affected by their having been born into a poor and, usually, not fully educated family.

One of the most difficult problems faced by minorities in America is racism. This is the case because so many of America's poor are blacks and Hispanics. Racism is the belief that racial groups display both physical and behavioral differences from the majority group in a society and that these differences are inherited. Related to this belief is that some of these differences are inferior and/or undesirable. Thus, prejudice is justified and unequal treatment of some racial groups—segregation, discrimination, and hostility—become excusable.

Racism is not the only problem for minorities. In America, many white people fall into the minority class. They too are victims of prejudice which is the act of prejudging someone based on stereotypes and hearsay rather than factual reasoning. It also comes from refusing to change your mind when confronted with sound and valid judgments and evidence. An example of poor, minority whites is a special group living in what is known as "Appalachia." These people, like other minorities, are poorly educated, clothed, fed, and housed. Unemployment among them is high and the jobs which they do hold are considered menial by the majority of whites in the area. This group is often referred to as "poor white trash;" a derogatory term reflecting prejudicial attitudes and discriminatory practices.

Cartoons

The two cartoons associated with this dilemma focus on these two minority groups which live in the United States. The first focuses on our nation's poor white population and the second, on our poor black population. Whereas prejudice refers to an attitude or a feeling, discrimination refers to the actions taken as a result of these attitudes and feelings. Discrimination is often personal—one on one—but most of the time it is institutional as in the cartoons that follow.

Questions related to cartoons:

1. What is your interpretation of the phrase "peace with honor" in the first cartoon?

2. What is the poverty income level for a family of four in the United States today?

3. Find out what minority groups fall into the poverty level in this country. Also, find out the following about them:

   a. average educational level for an adult in this class
   b. typical housing patterns for families in this class
   c. unemployment statistics for this class

4. Taking all this information into mind, write a position statement telling why you think these people remain our nation's poorest and most discriminated against group.

Discuss the following issues:

1. How can the United States justify its military budget when so many of its people live at or below the poverty level?

2. Research the growth patterns of classes in American society during the 20th century and the implications of these patterns for the next century.

3. If we define morality in terms of equality, freedom, and nondiscrimination, how can we say that America is a nation that believes in and supports the moral issues associated with human rights?

4. Find information about the group known as "Habitat for Humanity." What are their goals? their motives? their ideals? Do you believe that this is a worthy cause? Why? Why not?

"I THINK THEY CALL IT 'PEACE WITH HONOR!'"

2/6/73

"....AND WE WERE FED REGULARLY, AND THE HEATING WORKED, AND NO RATS AND..."

11/14/72

24

Mind Builder
Monopoly

The purpose of this exercise is to show students how economic discrimination adversely affects minorities.

1. Divide the class up into groups of six or eight (preferably an even number). Have a monopoly game for each group in the class.

2. Assign half the players in each group membership in a dark-skinned minority and the remaining half are whites.

3. Before beginning play, draw up a new set of rules that favor the whites. Different sets of Chance and Community Chest cards can be drawn up. Assign different fees for passing Go. Different standards or rules can be set up for going and getting out of jail. Set up some "Whites Only Neighborhoods."

4. Give students the opportunity to play the game from both sides.

5. Have students discuss their feelings after the game is completed. Do they have greater understanding of the problems faced by minorities in American society? What are the effects of discrimination on the targets of prejudice? What are the effects of prejudice and discrimination on those doing the discriminating?

Mind Builder
Occupational Prestige

The purpose of this exercise is to demonstrate the relationship between occupational prestige and social status.

1. The teacher is to list ten different occupations on the board.

2. Have students rank them from high to low.

3. Discuss each occupation in terms of the following:
    — salary and/or wages
    — amount of training or education needed
    — reputation of the person in the community
    — life style, such as leisure time activities, hobbies, dress, etc.

4. Are there any similarities in how the students ranked the occupations? Is there a clustering tendency in ranking some of the occupations? If so, does this represent class distinctions?

DILEMMA DEBATE #4:
PEACE ON EARTH, GOOD WILL. . .

Is permanent peace possible? One of the most important, if not *the* most important moral and social dilemma of our time, is the relationship of nations to one another. Although no one can predict the future with any certainty, we may wonder if human beings are destined to move into an era of peace, goodwill, and international harmony; or, on the other hand, will more terrible wars threaten the future of generations yet to be born?

The cartoons connected with this dilemma raise an important question regarding the leadership of our country. From the President, who talks about promoting peace and goodwill on earth, to those toy makers who apparently control the thinking of many young people, peace and goodwill seem all too often lost for the sake of economic gain.

Mind Builder
Toys and War

The toys sold to our children can be viewed as a clue to society's values. Have students bring to class representatives of the different types of toys that they played with when they were younger, or that they still play with. Have the class discuss the traits of American life that coincide with these objects. A few illustrations are:

Toy Banks:
teach the value of thrift and saving. Elements of the Protestant Ethic remain in our culture.

War Toys:
express the values of heroism, hostility, sexism, strength, and aggression. You may wish to emphasize these toys with this exercise.

Superhero Dolls:
express the value of justice through providing good-guy role models for the young; they also contain the value of self-determination by expressing a child's need for power and autonomy in a world ruled by adults.

Discussion

1. What are some of the problems we face as a nation seeking to make democracy effective at home and seeking peace and justice in foreign affairs?

2. Does a large supply of nuclear weapons make peace on earth a closer reality?

3. Are there any human rights that are morally above national rights? If so, what are they?

4. Do we need an international code of ethics for space travel, space exploration, and space weapons?

5. How would you evaluate the statement: "There is no alternative to peace except utter destruction?"

"EUREKA! WE FINALLY DEVELOPED A NUCLEAR WEAPON!...NOW WE DINOSAURS WILL RULE THE EARTH FOREVER!"

DILEMMA DEBATE #5:
THE NATURE OF PREJUDICE

In the last problem we observed that prejudice and discrimination usually go hand-in-hand. But they can occur independently of each other. For example, a person may retain his or her belief that all Spanish-speaking people are drug dealers. If, in spite of this belief, that person lets Spanish-speaking people move into his or her neighborhood without interference, s/he is displaying prejudice without discrimination. Any effort to block them from moving into the neighborhood would be prejudice with discrimination. On the other hand, a person may think that his/her neighbors are ridiculous for believing such slanderous things about Spanish-speaking people. Because one does not, however, want the neighbors as enemies, s/he freely signs a petition to keep them out of the neighborhood. This is discrimination without prejudice.

In general, prejudice and discrimination are mutually reinforcing. Most prejudices among people are acted on either personally or institutionally— they are put into the religious, educational, or legal system of the society. This result is discrimination. Today, most forms of discrimination have been legally abolished, but because many people have deep-seated prejudices, they have discovered ways to avoid full compliance with the law and thus, discrimination still flourishes among us.

Cartoons

In the first cartoon, a man (Senator Jesse Helms of North Carolina) demonstrates the inconsistencies which can arise because of conflicting prejudices. In the struggle over the issues of abortion and welfare, the result of his strident opposition to welfare and to abortion is contradictory for the unborn children. He is concerned to protect the right to life of the unborn child but will not do anything to help ensure that fetus is healthy, is properly cared for, or has adequate nourishment. Is there prejudice toward women in this position? What should we do as a nation which professes the highest degree of morality about women's rights?

In the second cartoon, we bumped head-on into two major fallacies in our reasoning processes, inconsistency (self-contradiction) and name calling (attacking the person rather than the argument). Are the attitudes expressed in this cartoon consistent with Christian ethics? Do they show prejudice? What we seem to need is a method for retaining our consistency in argumen-

tation and a way of keeping our emotions in check as the debates begin to
heat up.

Activity:

When we focus on equal rights for women, two major issues often come
to the top of our thinking: abortion and salary discrimination. Using the
problem-solving strategies outlined in Section One of this book, choose one
of these issues, divide the class into research teams, and seek a group
solution to these problems. As you reach your final solutions and bring them
into the class for discussion, refer to the section in this book entitled,
"Planning For Classroom Discussion." Following the steps and ideas pro-
vided for you in these sections will help you avoid fallacious arguments and
discover more useful and acceptable solutions.

When you have finished with this activity, answer the following questions:

1. In your research, did you carefully seek out factual information or did
   you "doctor" the facts to suit your preconceived purposes?

2. While debating with other members of the class, did you keep your
   emotions in check? That is, did you avoid name calling, screaming,
   and the like?

3. Did you follow the problem-solving method outlined in Section One
   of this book? Did you document each step along the way? Did it work
   for you?

4. Was the class solution a compromise of differing positions or did one
   group dominate? Explain your answer to this question.

5. Were you personally satisfied with the solution agreed upon by the
   class? If not, what changes would you make in it?

"CRACKPOT!"

12/6/7

MEMO

TO: APOSTLE PAUL
FROM: MACHISMOS OF MACEDONIA
RE: WOMEN PRIESTS
    DEAR PAUL:
    HANG TOUGH ON THIS FEMALE ISSUE.
    AFTER ALL, NONE OF CHRIST'S APOSTLES ARE WOMEN.
    ALSO ONLY JEWS SHOULD BE PRIESTS BECAUSE NO
    APOSTLES ARE GENTILES.   FURTHERMORE, ONLY
    SHORT, BEARDED PEOPLE

Mind Builder
Who Should Be Spared?

The purpose of this exercise is to have students think about their values and beliefs about what is desirable for a person to do and be in American society.

Ten people are trapped on the top of a skyscraper which is on fire. There is only one possible escape route: a small tunnel leading to safety. Only one person at a time can enter the tunnel and crawl to safety. Not very much time is left for the group to escape.

The task of the students is to arrange the people below in the order they would have them escape. Remember that at any time the escape route may be closed.

Let the students work individually on the problem. Have them carefully and systematically record their thoughts about why they lined the people up as they did.

Arrange the students in groups to discuss their solution and the reasons for their choices.

— Are some people consistently at the front of the line and others at the end of the line?

— Discuss what might be the reasons for this.

— What does this tell us about status and prestige in American society?

— What, if any, were the assumptions made about these people?

People on Top of the Skyscraper:

Television preacher	Pregnant female
Small child	Congressman
Businessman	Professional athlete
Policeman	Engineer
Famous poet	Medical doctor

DILEMMA DEBATE #6:
THE FIRST AMENDMENT

Life forces both individuals and human groups to make value judgments. Valuing occurs whenever anything—a physical object, a way of acting, an idea, or a person—is preferred or chosen. We rate things and circumstances as better or worse and act on these decisions and ratings. As we study the historical struggles of our past, we discover that certain values and, hence, certain rights were considered fundamental. Anyone who talks to the person on the street will discover that s/he cherishes certain rights which s/he believes should be recognized and protected.

Since World War II, three documents have appeared which are of special significance in the discussion of human rights. The first was published in 1947 and depicts the struggle for human rights in the United States up to that time. *To Secure These Rights* shows that the struggle for human rights is far from over, even in democratic countries. In 1960, there appeared a report of the President's Commission on National Goals entitled, *Goals for America*. This second document defines the values that can become the basis of further revisions in our view of human rights in American society. The third document which appeared during this time is, *The Universal Declaration of Human Rights,* and is worldwide in its scope and significance.

By the end of the decade of the 1980s, standards set by these documents will have been written into law and not just in America. They will have appeared in many national constitutions. These documents and declarations have become the moral standards for outlawing genocide, abolishing slavery, and promoting equal rights among men and women. Using these documents as a motivating force, over fifty colonial territories have gained self-government.

Today, men and women and boys and girls make claims on governments and social organizations involving fundamental human rights. Minorities, ethnic groups, children, the aged, and women have and are making claims on the majority group in power. Some call these rights "natural," others call them "God-given," and still others call them just "human rights." No matter what they are called, they have been instrumental in our development and fundamental to our future. They are founded on the perceived nature of man and on the conditions necessary for the development of people's potentials. Human rights represent the conditions of life without which a person cannot live at his or her best.

34

Activities:

1. Secure copies of the three documents mentioned in this dilemma and prepare a summary for class discussion.

2. Study American life since World War II and identify the elements in our society which hinder the development and expression of fundamental human rights.

3. Below is a listing of fundamental human rights. Study this list and give your reasons for accepting or rejecting any of the rights mentioned.
    a. The right to health
    b. The right to education
    c. The right to freedom
    d. The right to work and receive a better wage
    e. The right to security
    f. The right to live in a home
    g. The right to recreation and leisure
    h. The right to share in controlling one's life
    i. The right to share your cultural heritage
    j. The right to worship

Discussion:

1. Reread the Constitution of the United States. List the rights guaranteed in its amendments. How well are these rights recognized and followed in America today? (Give particular attention to Amendments I, V, XIV, and XV.)

2. Study the cartoons in this dilemma. Answer: What is the value of our basic freedoms? What is the value of having such a Constitution?

3. Are the rights which you selected above guaranteed by the Constitution? Why are they so valued? If they are not valued, reevaluate your choices and give reasons for any changes which you might have made.

"DISGUSTING!" "OBSCENE!" "WITHOUT REDEEMING SOCIAL VALUE!"

6/25/73

Mind Builder
Being Different

The purpose of this exercise is to show students that what they wear (their appearance) influences how they respond to others and others respond to them.

1. Have students wear something different to school. The change in dress style should be obvious to others. For example, if a student usually dresses very neatly, this student should dress in sloppy clothes. If a student dresses sloppy, this student should dress extremely neat.

2. Have students take notes of the differences in how people responded to them. At the end of the school day have students discuss the experience.

3. Discuss the following questions: What types of questions did other students or teachers ask? Why did they ask the questions? Were other students surprised? How did you feel out of your customary dress? Do our clothes send nonverbal messages to people? What kind of messages?

DILEMMA DEBATE #7:
BEING HUMAN

In our efforts to honor, protect, and live up to the mandates of the United States Constitution, we will do well to consider each right separately and ask if it is adequately recognized and safeguarded in the present social order. In our drive for fame, fortune, and happiness, human values and human welfare are often forgotten.

For anyone to have a right, there must be someone—an individual, a group, a society, or a government—who has an obligation or duty to see that each person is protected in these rights. Rights mean that we also have obligations. To be and to act fully human means that we will responsibly recognize the rights of ourselves and others.

For example, while a child as a person has rights, the child's parents have a special responsibility for the child's care while he or she is a dependent. Society and governments hold the parent accountable for such care and may, in extreme cases, place the child in the care of others when these obligations are not fulfilled.

If all persons have the right to life, liberty, and the pursuit of happiness, then they also have corresponding duties to respect the lives of others, to refrain from infringing on their liberties and to refrain from placing avoidable obstacles in the way of their happiness. Thus, for every right there is an obligation.

Obligation networks, like human rights, must be measured by the situation in which they are applied and function to foster the betterment of human life. Obligations arise from the interactions of humans with each other. When conflicts between persons occur, the solution should be directed in the interest of the greater achievable net values. Being human means that when we make decisions that we take into consideration the needs of persons involved in the consequences of that decision, the values at stake in the decision, and the circumstances that will bear on the decision.

Activities:

1. Below is a list of our decision-making obligations. Study the list carefully and add to it or take from it as you think it ought to be amended. Please justify your choices.

    a. One is obligated to meet his or her responsibilities with due care. That is, one must evaluate each short-and long-range consequence of his or her decision-making as to how it will affect others and as to its consistency with respect to morality.

b. One is obligated to be well-informed. To do right one must first know right, including an awareness of the law, an understanding of the general demands of good conduct, knowledge of one's own motives and intentions, and of the consequences of the alternatives being considered.

c. The obligation to act diligently on one's knowledge. The other half of knowing one's obligations is applying that knowledge in morally consistent ways. In his book, *The Meaning of Right and Wrong*, Richard C. Cabot tells us that...

> One is responsible morally as well as legally for blunders: (1) up to the limits of average intelligence, or the intelligence to be expected in the individual concerned; and (2) except in situations where one could not reasonably have been expected to foresee and prepare for.

2. What moral issues are involved in the following situations (explain your answers):

a. The setting off of a false fire alarm at school.

b. Hunting on land that is posted "No Hunting."

c. Selling a used car with a defective part without informing the buyer that the part is defective.

d. Driving a motorized vehicle while drinking alcoholic beverages.

3. Write ten rules for parents which you think they should definitely follow. Give your reasons for these rules.

4. The two cartoons in this dilemma represent obligation networks.

a. In the first cartoon, why do you think George's wife makes these remarks to her friend? What kind of person do you think George is? Would you like to have George as a father? Why? Why not?

b. In the second cartoon, we witness the violation of moral obligation. Read Orwell's *Animal Farm*. Once you have read this book, explain the concept of "totalitarianism." What, in your opinion, is meant by the phrase, "...But some are more equal than others." Can you find evidence that some people indeed act this way in our own culture? Do you think that some people are "more equal" than others? Justify your explanation.

"THEY RECALLED THE TIRES, THE CAR, THE TV, THE FOOD, THE MICROWAVE—
I FIGURE IF I'M PATIENT SOONER OR LATER THEY'LL GET AROUND TO GEORGE!"

Mind Builder
Equality/Inequality

For several days have students observe closely the behavior of several people with whom they spend a considerable amount of time. Have students look for situations where these people by word or gesture exhibit racial or ethnic prejudice. Have students describe in detail several of the situations they observed.

For Class Discussion:

- Do you think the person was aware that s/he was expressing prejudiced attitudes?

- Would that person have said or done the same thing if a minority group member had been present?

- How would the person have responded if the student had told him or her that his or her behavior seemed prejudiced?

- Has the student behaved in a similar way? Does the student consider himself/herself prejudiced?

"....BUT SOME ARE MORE EQUAL THAN OTHERS." — ORWELL'S 'ANIMAL FARM'

SECTION THREE
DEFINING ETHICS

"Ethics" or "Morals" represents an entirely different field than the empirical sciences. Although ethics is interpersonal, having to do with human attitudes and behavior, it can be objective. The objectivity of our valuing depends upon our commitment to persons as valuable human beings, our commitment to reason objectively and consistently, and our willingness to reconsider different points of view.

As we enjoin the task of explaining and understanding our moral foundations, there are two considerations which we need to take into account as we define and make clear the concept of "morality." First, we need to think functionally about moral judgments. Some moral principles will hold by virtue of other facts. A behavior may be wrong because of some other features it has; for instance, the behavior may cause needless suffering to ourselves or others or it may betray the trust of a friend. The moral features of a behavior are not independent of other features of the act, but are implied by it. The answer to our question, "How is 'value' related to 'fact'?" will be discovered—in part—in the effects of the behavior on other human beings and on ourselves.

Secondly, morality is intrinsically related to the value or preciousness of persons and other living things. That is, we define certain behaviors as moral or immoral by the effects these behaviors have on persons and these effects in turn assist us in formulating our conception of morality. What we need to understand is that your value by virtue of your being a living being generates a moral claim on my behavior toward you and your behavior toward me. This idea, the idea of human value, is the very essence of morality. At the heart of morality lies such human conceptions as equality, justice, and nondiscrimination which form moral obligation networks, which permeate or ought to permeate our transactions with each other and our attitudes toward ourselves and other living beings.

The dilemma debates in this section of our book will assist our students in uncovering these ideas and applying the concept of morality to their personal and social decision-making. Such moral concepts as honesty, human equality, respect for life, our attitudes toward others, and the responsibility of government and industry will be explored with the purpose of exposing the underlying moral dimensions of human societal living.

Mind Builder
A Look at My Values

The purpose of this exercise is to encourage students to think about what kind of persons they are by looking at some things that are important to them.

1. Each student is to bring to class a plain T-shirt, no markings or symbols. A light colored shirt would work best.

2. Students are to design their own T-shirt by following the directions below: (Use magic markers and water colors.)

    — On the back of the T-shirt at the top the student will write a personal motto; the fewer words, the better.

    — On the back of the T-shirt below the motto, draw a design or symbol that illustrates the motto.

    — On the front of the T-shirt at the top, write the name of the job or occupation you have as a future goal.

    — On the front of the T-shirt below the occupation, draw a design or symbol of one thing that makes you happy now.

    — On the front of the T-shirt below the symbol, write the one word that best describes you as a person.

3. Have students discuss with one another their T-shirts. What do the shirts say about the student as a person? What messages does the shirt give off?

4. The teacher may want to have students vote on the best T-shirt. Judging should be based on originality and the degree to which the shirt fits the student's personality.

In this book we have studied many contemporary moral dilemmas and have made some efforts to solve or come to grips with them. Throughout we have talked about *morals* and *ethics* as judgments where the ideas of right and wrong may enter. Morality includes all forms of personal and social behavior.

Two other concepts which need mentioning and that are related to morals are the *law* and *professional ethics*. The law is a command of the state. It applies to all people who are citizens of the state and provides penalties for disobedience. The purpose of the law is the regulation of human behavior within a society, and it includes the settlement of conflicts between individuals.

Professional ethics refers to the codes of conduct of a particular profession. It provides for a person's professional privileges and regulates his or her professional responsibilities. Its purpose is like that of the law, i.e., to regulate the behavior of individuals who are members of a particular professional group.

Discussion

1. Study the Marlette cartoon in this section. Is Marlette accusing the two people in this cartoon of breaking a moral, legal, or professional standard of conduct? What do you think? Give your reasons.

2. It has been suggested that physical strength, personal beauty, pleasure, material things, money, political power, and the spiritual have all been worshipped in our society. Do you agree?

    Define the word *worship*. Given the definition of this word, which of the above—in your opinion—have been worshipped more than the others in contemporary society?

"TAKE ALL THAT YOU HAVE AND GIVE UNTO THE POOR, AND COME, FOLLOW ME!"

One aspect of the contemporary community is its mixture of people. In such societies people have the opportunity to interact with those who are different. However, all too often, such interaction breeds conflict rather than harmony. Often, two different racial groups may be in conflict.

When there is intergroup conflict in a society, one group is dominant and usually has control over the other group, which is in the minority. The minority group is the group which receives unequal treatment.

The unfair or unequal treatment of people—usually because of sex, race, nationality, or religion—is termed "discrimination." It is prejudice that often causes discrimination. "Prejudice" is an unfair or false belief about a group of people. When one person or group is prejudiced toward another, the group or person that is prejudiced usually considers the other group inferior or undesirable. Action which results from prejudice is discrimination.

Discussion

In the two cartoons on the following page, Doug Marlette reacts to institutional racism—a form of prejudice and discrimination—which has become an integral part of our society because of its historical support by the dominant groups.

1. In small groups, study the two cartoons. Discuss to what extent the two cartoons reflect the feelings of group members.

2. In the first cartoon, Paul Revere is warning the citizens of Boston. Why? Has this warning been heard in other communities?

3. Why do you think people have prejudiced attitudes? Can you identify any in yourself? List some of them.

4. In the second cartoon we have a reference to both the North and the South. Develop a project in which you show the differences in how racism is expressed in the North and the South. Include in this project any steps that have been taken to remove or reduce prejudiced attitudes in people.

46

"THE COLOREDS ARE COMING! THE COLOREDS ARE COMING!"

"OH, I WISH I WAS IN THE LAND OF COTTON...."

Mind Builder
Social Distance Scale

The purpose of this exercise is to allow students to investigate their own negative feelings about certain groups.

1. Have students work independently during the first part of this exercise.

2. Following is a list of groups students may have some negative feelings about and a list of possible relationships. Inform students to react to the group as a whole and not to the best or worst individual they may have known in the group.

3. The student is to check the box that most accurately reflects his/her feelings about the group. Only one box is checked for each group.

	1	2	3	4	5	6	7
Blacks							
Whites							
Mexicans							
Puerto Ricans							
Cubans							
Indians							
Jews							
Catholics							
Protestants							
Moslems							

(1) Would have as best friend (2) Would have as neighbor (3) Would have as classmate (4) Would allow in community (5) Would allow in my state (6) Would allow in my country (7) Would not allow in my country.

4. Total the numbers of the boxes checked to get your social distance score. (The higher the score the more rejecting a person is, and the lower the score the more accepting the person is.)

5. Organize the class into small groups (five or six) and discuss the reasons why certain groups were rejected more than others. Are these reasons valid?

Mind Builder
Birds of a Feather. . .

As the students file into class the teacher orders them to sit in special sections based on the student's religious affiliation. They must sit in their special section during the entire class. Students who challenge the system are ordered to sit in a separate section labeled "troublemakers."

1. The teacher may conduct some other classroom activities during this time, but there cannot be any communication or association among the various religious groups.

2. At a later time have students discuss the feelings they experienced being separated from others.

DILEMMA DEBATE #10:
RESPECT FOR LIFE

The ideals that a group of people feel are the best and most important are called "values." These values represent norms or standards of behavior. They can represent the ideals of an entire society, or of only a small segment of the society. They tell people how to behave.

Some strong American values are patriotism, unselfishness, honesty, and truthfulness. You can find these values in the Declaration of Independence, the Bill of Rights, and the Ten Commandments.

Discussion

The next two cartoons represent how human ideals and values mesh with real human beings and real societal institutions. In the first cartoon we are reminded that there are few super heroes in real life. However, we should realize that there are many unselfish people who live heroic lives in our communities.

1. In small groups, discuss the distinction between selfish and unselfish behavior. What is the meaning of these concepts? List some examples of selfish and unselfish behavior you have observed in your community.

2. Do you believe that humans are by nature selfish or unselfish? Do you agree or disagree with most of your classmates on the nature of human beings?

The second cartoon also involves some of our society's institutions.

1. What opinions are being expressed in this cartoon?

2. The concept, "respect for life," is mentioned in this cartoon. What does this concept mean to you?

3. Write a short essay entitled, "Institutionalized Values in the Human Community." In small groups, discuss your views with other students.

There is a man who was sent to earth by his father, was raised in humble circumstances and since he was not of this world dwelt among men an outsider..... But his was a special destiny...... By dedicating his unique gifts to the service of truth and justice he stood for the oppressed, the meek, the afflicted, the powerless...... for all of humanity......
This is not Him.

THE TROUBLE WITH THOSE BACKWARD COUNTRIES IS THEY DON'T HAVE THE SAME RESPECT FOR LIFE THAT WE DO!'"

Mind Builder
Community and Societal Values

1. Have students locate such parlor games as *Monopoly* or *Life* and play the games several times in class. As the students are playing, encourage them to think about the following questions:

    a. What does the game teach about life in American society?

    b. What does the game teach about success or achievement in American society?

    c. What human or societal values do the games represent?

    d. Do the games accurately represent what is going on in your particular community?

Note: This project could be expanded to include video games. What do these games teach about life? About the community? About other countries?

DILEMMA DEBATE #11:
DOES THE SHOE FIT?

Prejudices are of many kinds. There are racial, class, religious, social, and sexist prejudices, just to name a few. A prejudice is a mental bias—an opinion held in disregard for the facts—that, when not kept in control, leads a person to make judgments without first examining all the evidence.

The concept that all human beings should enjoy equal rights and respect is not new to American ideology. But this principle has been violated time and again with respect to women.

Discussion

1. Carefully read the Marlette cartoon included in this activity. Notice how the "shoe is put on the other foot."

2. If you are a male, how does it feel to be stereotyped? Does it make you feel angry? Do you feel like you are not being treated fairly? How does it feel to be "pigeon-holed?"

Mind Builder
Short-Hand Perceptions

All of us have short-hand pictures of the people of other groups. These short-hand or limited perceptions are called stereotypes. A stereotype is an extreme generalization about members of a group. This is a simplistic view of the person(s) in question.

Comic Strip Analysis

Have students choose three older comic strips that represent people in social/professional life and three contemporary comic strips that represent people living today.

Follow these strips for at least one week.

a. Strip Analysis:
    — Are there differences in how women are depicted?
    — Are there differences in how older people are represented?
    — Are there any differences in the way children and teenagers behave and talk?

b. As a follow-up exercise, observe old and new TV shows and make a note of differences in the ways that different groups are depicted.

54

It is a well-documented fact that about 80% of the employed women in the U.S. are in clerical, sales, factory, farm, or service occupations. Only 6% are medical or health workers. 5% are managers, officials and proprietors. Yet the United States Department of Labor finds women more reliable and less absent from their jobs than men.

Discussion

1. Why are many women in this country employed at levels lower than men? Why do women make less money at the same job than men?

2. What response to the plight of working women in this country do you advocate? Why?

3. Our society has already decided that people should get equal pay for equal jobs. An issue that is now being addressed is *equal pay for comparable work*. What does the term *comparable work* mean? Give examples.

What are the implications of Women's Rights? To understand this problem thoroughly, students may wish to trace the history of some of the major issues and events in the Women's Rights movement. Some students may wish to trace the history of the Civil Rights movement in the United States. When these two histories have been outlined, the class should be led through a careful comparison of the two. Are there similarities? What are the differences?

Discussion

1. Study Marlette's cartoon included below. Has the Women's Rights movement brought about some unanticipated results and changes in our society? List some of these changes.

2. How has the Women's Rights movement changed our way of life in the past 25 years?

3. At issue in the Women's Rights movement is how past injustices can be corrected and how discriminatory attitudes ingrained in the fabric of our culture can be rooted out.

   — Make a list of the most needed steps that would lead toward genuine equity among men and women.

   — Examine each of these steps. Will they lead to a removal of the real causes of inequity among men and women?

DILEMMA DEBATE #12:
PLAYING WITH DICE

Since the nuclear accidents at Three Mile Island and Chernobyl, many people have suggested that the government and nuclear power companies are taking unsafe chances with human lives. Their argument is that the safeguards that would protect human communities from the hazards of nuclear wastes are not in place.

Some people feel that long-term perspectives are needed: this world must be thought of in terms of its being preserved and maintained for those yet to be born.

Mind Builder
Nuclear Power: Blessing or Curse?

The purpose of this exercise is to acquaint students with the advantages and disadvantages of nuclear power.

1. Divide the class into pairs (dyads). Have one student prepare a short paper on the advantages of nuclear power, the other one on the disadvantages. An interesting twist here would be to have the student research the side of the question s/he feels the less committed to.

2. After the papers are completed, have the student present his findings to his partner. After some discussion of the papers, have the students in each dyad concatenate their findings into one final report.

3. Allow several pairs to present their findings to the class. Did anyone change his mind after doing the research or listening to the other reports?

4. Have students discuss what changes would occur in their community if there was no nuclear power. What if all the power was nuclear?

In the first of the subsequent cartoons, Marlette has created a picture of a "funny looking" nuclear plant. Study the cartoon carefully.

Discussion

1. In small groups, have the students discuss their individual interpretations of this cartoon. Have students state whether they agree or disagree with Marlette's views.

2. Invite a nuclear plant representative to class. Discuss with this official the problems of nuclear wastes, fallout, and what plans they have for the community in case of a nuclear accident.

In the second cartoon, Marlette suggests that the government and nuclear officials are actually covering up the dangers and hazards of nuclear power.

Discussion

1. Before you agree or disagree with Marlette's point of view, complete a short research paper on the accident at Three Mile Island or any other nuclear accident you can find out about.

    a. Have students find out what actually happened at these places.

    b. Why did it happen?

    c. How were these problems handled by the nuclear power officials at the time of the incident? How are they handled today?

2. In small groups, have the students discuss Marlette's point of view.

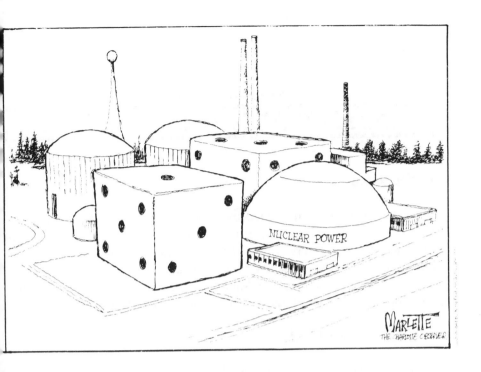

POLITICAL/SOCIAL VALUES

Introduction

Americans have been described by people from other countries as rich, spoiled, wasteful, and violent. It is true that the standard of living is high in America and, because of this fact, Americans appear to be a wasteful nation. Also, American history is filled with wars and other forms of violence. Today, the crime rate in America is high. Over one thousand people are now on death row in our nation's prisons waiting to be put to death.

Are We a Violent People?

Some say that the violence which characterizes much of American life is reflected in inner-city turmoil, crime, political cheating, and the treatment of convicted murderers. It has been suggested that a conflict is raging in the world today—America included. It is not a conflict between East and West or between Communism and Democracy. Rather, it is a conflict in the minds of people about ultimate values; about good and bad; right and wrong behaviors; and truth and honesty.

Before you begin this section of the book, complete the following activities:

1. Study the cartoon, "Openness." What values are being displayed in this cartoon? Are these values representative of American as well as Russian society? Explain and justify your answers.

2. Working in small groups, construct a set of values toward which individuals and societies ought to be working.

3. Would these values work on a world-wide basis? What assumptions did you make about the human condition in developing these ideal values?

"IT'S PART OF COMRADE GORBACHEV'S NEW 'OPENNESS'!"

Mind Builder
Advertising America

1. Have students write a brief description of three of their favorite television commercials.

2. Working in small groups, have students discuss their favorite commercials. What values of American life are reflected in these commercials? Could any of these be considered "ideal" values?

3. Have each group construct a profile of values drawn from the commercials presented by group members.

4. Compare these with the set of ideal values developed earlier in this section. What have you learned about values from this exercise?

DILEMMA DEBATE: #13:
JUSTIFYING ACTIONS

In the previous questions, the basic problem concerning capital punishment was whether society had a moral right to sanction the death of one of its members. Concerning this issue, good and reasonable people will disagree. Some believe that capital punishment is morally right for convicted killers. Others believe that no matter how heinous the crime, a true life sentence would be adequate.

Discussion

1. Before students state their beliefs on this issue, they should study the next cartoon. Here we see representatives from three different cultures, all giving their reasons for keeping the practice of capital punishment in their respective societies.

   a. What are their reasons? Might there be a difference between the *real* reasons and their publicly stated reasons? If so, why?

   b. Are their reasons sufficient to justify capital punishment?

   c. In small groups, students discuss their own beliefs on this issue.

2. The concept, "moral right," has been used in the debate over capital punishment.

   a. Have the students discuss what this concept means.

   b. Can it mean different things to different people? What problems does this create for a community? A society?

   c. Murder, in any society, is a lawless act. Is it possible for societies acting under the law to commit murder? If so, what might be some of these lawful acts? List and discuss.

Mind Builder
Till Death Do Us Part

1. Have students conduct interviews with the following people to discover their views on the death penalty.

    a. Pastor or Priest
    b. Policeman
    c. Business Executive

2. Interviews should include the following questions (have the students add their own questions to the ones below):

    a. In general, do they favor the death penalty? If so, what crimes should result in the death penalty?

    b. Have them state their positions on the death penalty from a religious point of view, from a moral point of view, and from a practical point of view.

    c. In small groups, have students discuss their feelings.

DILEMMA DEBATE #14:
LET THERE BE LIGHT

During the 1986-1987 debate on the virtues of Scientific Creationism and Evolution teaching in the public schools, the Supreme Court finally decided on June 20, 1987 that there should not be any particular religious point of view—which Creationism is—taught in state supported public schools. In Charlotte, North Carolina the reactions were mixed, but because Charlotte lies at the heart of the "Bible-belt," one expected reactions like the following:

> I think it should be left up to the local area. If the majority of people in a certain area feel that creationism should be taught, then they should be able to.

Others reacted to this comment:

> No matter how one evaluates this statement (referring to the comment above), it's an alarming idea. Logically speaking, this person is asking us to decide the validity of scientific fact and scientific hypotheses by popular vote. Can we decide that the world is flat by getting enough people to agree to it? Can we decide that certain human beings are inferior to others because some people say that they are?

The question which we need to ask ourselves is: "What was the Supreme Court decision about anyway?" The Court was asked to decide upon the constitutionality of a law which required publicly funded schools to teach "scientific" Creationism alongside evolutionary biology.

The Supreme Court had to...

1. Decide if Creationism is science or religion posing as science. They decided upon the latter.

2. Next, the Court was forced to rule that the teaching of creation science— a religious belief—was in violation of the principle of the separation of church and state.

Said one person, "What is at stake here is not whether communities and individuals are free to decide upon their own religious beliefs, but whether public money should be used to promote these beliefs."

64

ctivities:

Examine the cartoons in this dilemma. What message is the cartoonist sending to us in Cartoon #1; in Cartoon #2? Do you agree or disagree with his viewpoint? Explain and justify your answers.

Prepare a debate on this issue. Take the following reactions into consideration:

a.   The Court was wrong to ban Creationism because. . .

— an issue such as Creationism cannot die when it's supported by 86% of the population.

— teachers ought to be allowed to teach Creationism but not forced to do so.

— evolution is mere theory or explanation, not an established fact.

— creation science is scientific.

— proponents of evolution cannot explain from whence comes the inanimate materials from which life evolved.

— principles of academic freedom demand the investigation of every theory, even those of a religious nature.

b.   The Court was right to ban Creationism because. . .

— the Bible story is not scientific fact or scientific theory but religious belief.

— why just teach the Jewish/Christian belief, why not include all the world's religions?

— the First Amendment to the Constitution bars governments from establishing or supporting any religious point of view.

— if the schools teach a particular religious belief, then they put religious freedom in jeopardy for those millions who do not share this particular belief.

3. In your debate be sure to clarify any words or phrases which may ha unclear meanings and usages. Such concepts as scientific theor hypothesis, and fact need our careful attention.

"LET THERE BE LIGHT!"

Mind Builder
Separation of Church and State

The purpose of this exercise is to give students insight into the complex issues related to the separation of church and state doctrine.

Americans believe very strongly in the separation of church and state principle. In fact, this principle can be viewed as a dominant value in American society. However, total adherence to this value is virtually impossible because many norms and beliefs in non-religious areas have religious origins. Also, there are some societal norms and beliefs that some religious groups oppose.

1. Have students list several American laws or norms that are reinforced by religious institutions and indicate the specific religious principle for the law or norm.

2. Have students list several American laws or norms that are in conflict with the religious beliefs and norms of at least some of the religious groups in America.

3. Place samples of both lists on the board. Conduct a discussion on what these two lists tell us about the degree of separation of church and state in America.

4. Students can use their own religions in discussing this issue.

DILEMMA DEBATE #15:
IT'S BEEN ONE OF THOSE WEEKS

There are those who claim that a distinction must be made between individual moral standards and conduct, on the one hand, and the behavior of professional and social groups and organizations on the other hand. There are elements, they say, in man's collective behavior that cannot readily be brought under the guidance of reason and conscience. Relations between groups will be more ruthless than relations between individuals, especially where self-preservation (the profit motive, etc.) is at stake.

In the cartoons below, Marlette gives us an example of both types of these problems. In the cartoon, "Ban the Pit Bulls," the problem is placed squarely on the shoulders of the dog owners. This seems to be a simple problem: make a law and enforce it. Either put the dogs to death or put the dog owners in prison. We can even justify this position by reference to several moral postulates:

1. Do unto others as you want others to do to you.

2. Every person is an equal center of sentient experience whose rights and freedoms should not be infringed upon unnecessarily by others (pit bull dogs).

But the case of Delta Airlines, a large corporation, is somewhat more complicated. On the surface, it appears the same as the "bulldog" situation, but instead of involving just individuals, this situation involves groups of individuals who are in competition with one another.

Group selfishness is a dangerous kind of selfishness. While masquerading under the cloak of loyalty to one's group, a person may do much harm to other groups and to the welfare of society in general. Part of the problem of ethics is to help men free themselves from the bias of narrow self-interest and pressure of group opinion and to develop a concern for the welfare of the larger communities of which they are a part. "No man is an island," and the same can be said of any group (business, industry, civic organization, church or government).

Activities:

1. The economic system that prevails in the United States, Canada, and many other parts of the world is called capitalism or the free enterprise system.

68

Capitalism rests on four main doctrines:

a. The doctrine of free enterprise
b. The doctrine of competition
c. The doctrine of the profit motive
d. The doctrine of the right to private property

2. Plan a research project in which you. . .

— define and give examples of each of the above doctrines.

— state both the positive and negative effects of capitalism.

— outline some specific unethical practices which are a result of this system.

— suggest methods for improving the ethical standards of business and industry.

3. Here are some general criticisms of the capitalistic system. Can you give examples from your experience and reading of each of these?

a. Extreme and unjust equality

b. Waste and lack of planning from the human point of view

c. Overemphasis on the desire to make money

d. A lopsided society in which human welfare is disregarded because of the use of machines, the exploitation of nature, and the drive for power and profits.

e. Read the following books and discuss them in class:
Orwell, George—*Animal Farm, 1984*
Toffler, Alvin—*Future Shock, The Third Wave*

" IT'S BEEN ONE OF THOSE WEEKS!"

Mind Builder
Let the Liar Beware

The purpose of this exercise is to demonstrate to students the destructive affects lying has on relationships specifically, and on society in general.

1. Someone has said, "It is easy to tell a lie, but hard to tell only one." Arrange the students into groups and discuss this statement. Each group can report the highlights of its discussion to the entire class.

2. Have students report on an experience when someone lied to them.

    — Who lied to the student?

    — What was the lie?

    — What was the student's reaction when he found out the truth?

    — How did the lie affect the relationship with the liar?

3. Now have the students report on a "lying to" experience they do not mind revealing to the class.

    — To whom did the student lie?   .

    — What was the lie? Why did the student lie?

    — What was the student's reaction when the truth was discovered?

    — How did the lie affect the relationship with the person lied to?

(continued on the next page)

4. Have students discuss being "lied to" by advertisers, politicians, and other public figures. What are the effects of these so-called public lies?

   — Have students study advertisements on television or in magazines. Can they find any lies or half truths? Report these to the class.

DILEMMA DEBATE #16:
SUBWAY SEASON

With the recent shootings and subsequent trial of Mr. Goetz in New York City, the cries have gone out again for more gun control legislation. On the other side, there are those who oppose any type of gun control, especially the registration of guns and the limitation of purchasing handguns. On no other issue are emotions raised to so high a pitch when the discussion of these matters begins.

Now, man is a creature who distinguishes between what is and what ought to be. That is, man is a creature of reason. At times he feels a personal sense of responsibility to exert himself on behalf of what ought to be. Without the power of alternative choice, responsibility makes no sense to him. Sometimes when men and women are confronted with a choice of alternatives, they stop to deliberate on the nature of the alternatives presented and weigh carefully the reasons for and against each possible choice.

Those who wish little or no regulation of guns in American life claim that the majority of gun owners are rational and deliberate persons. They do not violate the rights of others and handle their weapons in a proper and safe manner.

Of course, what about the minority? A weapon in their hands is a license to rob or kill. They are not well educated and are therefore very irrational in their approach to confusing situations. They are apt to make bad choices. Should we license these people rather than guns?

You have heard it said that, "Guns don't kill, people do." Of course, it is people who created guns, carry guns, and use guns. Is it possible to regulate just who can purchase a gun in our society? How do we tell the sound reasoners from the unsound ones when they come into the gun store?

The arguments for and against gun control in American society eventually settle into an interpretation of the Second Amendment to the United States Constitution. It goes like this. . .

> A well-regulated militia, being necessary to the security of a free
> State, the right of the people to keep and bear arms, shall not be infringed.

In the Constitution, Amendment Two is the only Article that contains any explanation of why it was passed. It calls attention to a striking difference between the Constitution and the Declaration of Independence. The right to keep and bear arms was exceedingly precious to men who faced dangers of many kinds in their daily lives. Colonial farmers with their muskets had helped to win the Revolutionary War. On the frontier, a gun was usually the pioneer family's only protection against wild animals and prowling

Indians or thieves.

But times have changed. Some have argued that we do not need to bear arms for protection today because we are protected by local and state police authorities. Others argue that they need a loaded weapon in their homes for self preservation. Do they? Some contend that with the freedom to purchase weapons comes "freeway shootings," "subway shootings," and crimes of every sort imaginable. Do you agree?

And how about Amendment Two? What is the correct interpretation of this amendment? What did the framers of the American Constitution have in mind when they wrote Amendment Two into the law? For many, the issue is still open.

Activities:

1. Apply your problem solving skills to this dilemma. Research the history of interpretations and legislation concerning Amendment Two. Seek the most accurate interpretation of this law that is possible.

2. Study Marlette's cartoon carefully. He seems to be telling us something about the outcome of the Goetz trial in New York. What is it?

3. Do you think that the freeway shootings in California have any connection to the outcome of the Goetz trial? State your reasons and share them with the class.

4. Finally, finish this section with a class debate on whether to limit the buying of handguns or to keep things as they are.

"SUBWAY SEASON!"

Mind Builder
Gun Control. . .

The purpose of this exercise is to encourage students to investigate the opposing sides in the "right to bear arms" issue.

Strategy:

1. Divide the class into two groups. One group will represent the position of the right to bear arms. The other group will represent the position opposing the right to bear arms.

2. Each group is to give indepth research to their respective position utilizing. . .

   magazines
   editorials
   information from the NRA
   Constitution & federal
       legislation

   periodicals
   interviews
   state & local laws
   law enforcement agencies

3. Each group is to file a written report of their findings as well as prepare to defend their position in an open debate. (Group members are encouraged to prepare posters, signs, buttons, and other materials advertising their position.)

4. A spokesman for each group is to be selected to represent the group's views. Other teachers and school officials can be invited to judge the debate.

5. After the debate is over, both sides should sit down together and formulate a solution to this problem. Both positions should be summarized with assistance of the teacher pointing out main points and keeping the procedure on track.

DILEMMA DEBATE #17:
WHAT OUGHT TO BE DONE?

Our great-grandparents lived in a society that was predominantly rural, agricultural, individualistic, and self-sufficient. Today, we live in a world that is urban, industrial, complex, interdependent, and characterized by its quickness of change. Because the change from rural to urban came upon our parents so quickly, many found it difficult to adjust their thinking and shift their values to contemporary ways of living.

In past generations, human responsibility was primarily limited to a person's immediate family and friends. Today, the concept of *responsibility* has been expanded to include those groups and organizations upon which we are all dependent, as well as to those generations who are to follow us into this world.

In our changing world we have lost sight of many of the values of yesterday. Such values included honesty, justice, courage, and self-control. Today we need to build upon these values and construct a world characterized by such values as cooperation, a willingness to share, tolerance, open-mindedness, a concern for all individuals as people, and a desire to conserve the resources and beauty of nature.

As the dilemma in this section is discussed and debated, these values can be used as a standard by which to evaluate the behavior of people, groups, and organizations. As you work through this dilemma, you may want to make a composite listing of the many trends which are altering the way we live today. Organizing these trends under value headings will help your students gain a perspective on the characteristics of contemporary society.

One important need in our society is the need for developing and maintaining high standards of operation in corporations and industries. Such standards will concern the relationship of business to both the public interest and the general welfare of all people. The cartoon connected with this social dilemma expresses a viewpoint about the textile industry. This industry is one of the largest employers in the Southeastern United States. For years, this industry has produced clothing, linens, drapes, thread, and yarn. But Marlette has recognized another product of the textile industry: Brown Lung.

Discussion

1. Can you find the medical definition of "Brown Lung?" How many people have been affected by this disease?

2. How has the textile industry handled this problem?

3. Can you name some similar problems that affect other industries Examples can include acid rain, nuclear waste, etc. Find out mor about one of these problems. What are its causes? Its effects? Wha industries are involved? What are they doing about it?

4. Watch the movie *Silkwood*. What was the problem? How was it hand led? What happened to Karen Silkwood?

5. Write an essay entitled, "The Moral Responsibility of Business an Industry." Share your written work with a local newspaper.

Famous Products of the Textile Industry

CLOTHING   LINENS   DRAPES   BROWN LUNG

Mind Builder
American Values: Time Capsule

So far in this book, you have been given the opportunity to analyze the values and beliefs that characterize contemporary American Culture. Now it is time to build a more permanent record of your thoughts and your efforts. This is what you are to do:

1. Bring to class several artifacts which you believe represent your society.

2. Discuss these artifacts with members of your class. Explain why you think your artifacts are representative of your society.

3. Compare these artifacts with others you have studied which represent older cultures, such as the ancient Greeks, the Egyptians, or Americans in the 1920's.

4. As a class, select the artifacts which are to be placed in a time capsule and secured on your school grounds. Insert a letter with the artifacts which explains what these items represent. Place a copy of the letter in the school vault, and a note which locates the position of the time capsule.

5. At your tenth year high school reunion, open the time capsule, read the letter, and compare your past with your present.

6. After the time capsule has been secured in its resting place, students are to discuss any insights that the exercise brought about concerning American society.

UNRESOLVED ISSUES

Introduction

Aristotle defined man as a thinking being, and reflective thinking or critical intelligence has usually been listed among the unique qualities of persons. In every generation there have been attempts to influence persons or limit man's thinking and the expression of true opinion. Today, as yesterday, the struggle for freedom marches on.

In this book of political cartoons and exercises, we have put our faith in the value of critical thinking and informed judgment. We have tried to convey this feeling to you and your students. Most of the dilemmas discussed herein are unresolved. For this reason, we must teach our students to think and then to apply intelligence to social purposes. This, in our judgment, is the ethical function of education. It is an ongoing task.

Some Obstacles to Critical Thinking...

If human beings are truly "wise" or thinking beings, and if there is an obligation to be significantly informed and to exercise prudential reasoning, why is it that few persons live truly intelligent lives? Why is it that even in a society that praises freedom, there are obstacles within the lives of persons and in society to the free exercise of intelligence? Here are some answers to these questions, answers which each of us needs to take seriously in our own lives:

1. We are largely creatures of habit. Habits usually assist us with life's routine details, but hinder us when dealing with the new and unfamiliar.

2. Another obstacle to thinking is prejudice. A prejudice is a judgment in advance without adequate examination.

3. A third obstacle to thinking is propaganda, which is the spread of any belief or doctrine by methods which are not necessarily open and honest. It also refers to the spread of misinformation with indirect methods and selfish motives.

4. Finally, the pressure of public opinion is a fourth obstacle to thinking. Public opinion is easily swayed by emotion and tends to thrive on stereotypes or slogans and the opinions of people who have prestige.

During our lifetime the freedom of thought and expression has come under attack in many different areas. In the field of education, teachers have been dismissed for discussing such topics as civil liberties, race relations, labor relations, communism, and secular humanism. Freedom of thought and expression has been violated by the banning of speakers who represent minority viewpoints. The issue of censorship has been a persistent one in recent decades causing problems in public schools and public libraries. Freedom of thought and expression in the area of security clearance for those who work for the government or for those trying to get into America has been a problem for years. It seems that one must believe as the dominant group believes or else give up these freedoms. Finally, investigating committees of various governmental agencies have tended to ignore the important principle of the separation of powers as these committees have acted as prosecutors, juries, and judges as well as investigators.

Ask yourself these questions:

1. Would I permit other people to express views that are apparently true but that are opposed to my beliefs?

2. Would I permit others to say what I consider false but more or less harmless?

3. Would I permit others to express views that I believe to be both false and harmful?

If you cannot say "yes" to the above questions, then you do not really believe in freedom of speech. Before completing this book, you need to reconsider the value of critical expression and free thought in your society. Is it important to you?

DILEMMA DEBATE #18:
BAN THOSE BOOKS

While freedom is one of the basic human rights and values, it is not an absolute. There are other values and rights that need to be recognized and protected. My freedom ends where it brings injury to you. We all have heard it said that no one has a right to shout "fire" in a crowded theater. Such principles as "the public interest" and the "common good" are basic in free democratic societies. This is a dilemma where there will always be some differences of opinion and opposing views. Some controls are dangerous and repressive; others are beneficial and needed.

In the history of mankind, censorship and other forms of control have been more harmful than beneficial and have retarded man's development as a moral creature. Some individuals and groups have been convinced that they alone know what is true and what is good, and they have used their power in an attempt to control the rest of the population. Governments, churches, and other extremist groups have, in the past, are trying in the present, and will try again in the future, to keep everyone's peace of mind by banning what they do not like or what is new and different.

In recent times, the chief controversy has centered around the public schools and books. Outside the schools, certain other materials—films, books, and movies—are also under attack. Most parents feel that they need to control what their young children read, hear, and see, at least until the child has the maturity and the opportunity to develop some inner control.

But, how much freedom and how much control is desirable in the interest of the common good? Opinion polls indicate that a majority of the people in the United States do want censorship of some sort applied against obscenity and probably the details of gruesome crimes and violence. But just what is obscene material? This is a question often debated.

In 1986, the book, *Flowers For Algernon* was removed from public school libraries across this nation because some said that it contains "pornographic" material. In one school district, the demand was made that a values committee be appointed to review each book used in the public schools of that district. This committee, in tune with community values, would keep some books, censor other books, and put warning labels on still other books which could only be read with parental permission.

In response to this suggestion, the local newspaper said that...

> In a world filled with the sordid, the difficult, and the controversial, education's task is not to protect students by carefully shielding them from unpleasant reality, but to guide them in the growth and knowledge that will allow them to protect themselves.

Questions for Discussion:

1. How does the caption of this cartoon relate to what the book is actually about?

2. What interpretation can you give to the symbolism of this cartoon?

3. According to the local newspaper cited above, what is education's major purpose?

4. In your opinion what is the difference between literature that is pornographic and material that handles sexual themes in a realistic and appropriate fashion?

5. What is your opinion about having to read materials in school that disagree with your basic values and beliefs?

Activities:

1. Write an editorial that is either pro or con with reference to censorship.

2. With the assistance of your teacher, find out what books and other materials have been banned from your school district, in your state, and in the nation. Also, find out why they were banned. After reviewing this list or reading the materials, would you censor these books? Justify your response.

3. Write a paper responding to the following statement: "The control and the censorship of human communication are highly questionable, potentially dangerous, and occasionally necessary."

" IT'S JUST AWFUL—IT'S ABOUT THIS SLOW-WITTED FELLA WHO LEARNS TO THINK!"

84

Mind Builder
Censorship: Book Banning

The purpose of this exercise is to acquaint students with the basic issues related to censorship.

1. Have the students read *Huckleberry Finn*. Many of the students will have already read the book, but have them reread it for this exercise.

2. Divide the class into two groups. One group is to take the position that *Huckleberry Finn* is a major literary work and is to put together a report on the merits of the book. A second group is to take the position that the book is harmful to young people. This group is to put together a report on the book's harmful affect on young people.

3. Conduct a class discussion on the censorship issue.
    — What kinds of materials should be censored?
    — Who should decide on what can be seen or read?
    — Is there a difference in what should be censored in reading materials and what should be censored on television or in the movies?

4. Have students make a list of materials, literature, television programs, movies, etc., that they think should be censored and have them tell why.

DILEMMA DEBATE #19:
DRUG ABUSE

Any discussion of physical and mental health would be incomplete without a consideration of the use of alcohol, tobacco, and narcotics or soft—alcohol, smoking tobacco, and smokeless tobacco—and hard—narcotics, such as crack, cocaine, marijuana, hashish, hallucinogens, amphetamines, barbiturates, and heroin—drugs.

In this field we need clear thinking. In the past, many of the issues have been clouded by high emotion or confused propaganda. When we ask, "Does the use of certain substances affect life beneficially or adversely?", we need scientific evidence in order to answer the question adequately. Also, when we inquire into the ethical or unethical use of required drug testing for athletes, pilots, teachers, and other government employees, the issue centers around the discussions which we previously have had about human rights and basic freedoms.

The latter of the above questions is the most difficult to answer. People value and cherish their freedom and liberty. They resent outside interference into their personal lives. Another question to which we must give our attention is, "When our lives are both public and private, and when we make our living in the public sector, should not the protection of the public good be one of our highest goals?" No one will deny that mental and physical health are important. Thus, drug abuse—soft and hard—should be important to us and our society. What can be done about drug abuse and addiction? Should we consider victims of drug abuse sick persons needing medical attention?

More Questions for Consideration:

1. What is the justification for the government's enforcement of severe penalties against the use of hard drugs and then, not only condoning but profiting from the use of alcohol and tobacco?

2. The Narcotics Addict Rehabilitation Act of 1986 gives adults a choice of treatment instead of imprisonment if no other crime is involved. Do you agree with this law or disagree with it? Justify your response.

3. Speaking about a drug habit, a teenager was heard saying, "I think it is injurious, but I don't think a moral issue is at stake." Is this attitude prevalent? Do you agree with it or disagree with it? Why?

4. In the Mind Builder, "Dangerous Drugs," you are asked to rank the nine drugs included with this section in order of their relative danger. When you finish this task, state a punishment beside each of these drugs for (1) use of, and (2) sale of. Justify your responses.

5. There are two cartoons with this section. In the first, a mother is checking her child before bedtime. She checks the child's hands, face, and ears for cleanliness. Then she takes a urinalysis for purposes of checking for drug use. Do you think that the drug problem is that bad in America? Do you think that the drug problem will get that bad before it is cured? Do you think that the parent is violating the child's basic human rights? Give answers and justify your responses to these questions.

6. In the second cartoon, the reference is being made to the abuse of "over-the-counter" and/or prescription (legal) drugs. Research this problem. Answer: What percentage of Americans are addicted to these types of drugs and what can be done about it?

" PSSST—HAVE A VALIUM! "

Mind Builder
Dangerous Drugs

The purpose of this exercise is to encourage students to think about and discuss the dangers of taking drugs.

1. Nine drugs are listed below. Each student is to work independently and rank the nine drugs in the order of their relative dangers. Place a "1" by the most dangerous drug, the number "2" by the next most dangerous drug, and so on; "9" being the least dangerous of the nine.

2. As the student works through the exercise, s/he is encouraged to write down his/her ideas as to why s/he ranked each drug as s/he did.

3. The students should take the following criteria into account in deciding how to rank each drug:
    — being used repeatedly or compulsively
    — being taken intravenously
    — producing physical dependence
    — impairing judgment
    — causing social deterioration (not being able to hold a job)
    — producing irreversible tissue damage and disease
    — causing accidental death from overdose

4. Have students rank order the following drugs:

    _____ alcohol

    _____ barbiturates and hypnotics

    _____ tobacco smoking

    _____ glue sniffing

    _____ speed (methamphetamine and dexedrine)

    _____ heroin, codine, morphine, ana other opiates

    _____ marijuana

    _____ cocaine

    _____ LSD and other hallucinogens

ANSWER TO MIND BUILDER EXERCISE

Item	Experts' Ranking	Your Ranking	Difference Score
Alcohol	1		
Barbiturates & hypnotics	2		
Tobacco smoking	8		
Glue sniffing	5		
Speed (methamphetamine & dexedrine)	4		
Heroin, codeine, morphine, & other opiates	6		
marijuana	9		
cocaine	3		
LSD & other hallucinogens	7		
Total			

DILEMMA DEBATE #20:
THE BUCK STOPS ELSEWHERE

American citizens look to their government for security, for justice, and for services that exceed their capacity or the capacity of the private sector in general to provide. We are most vividly aware that the social and political institutions under which men live profoundly affect their lives. The government has final authority within a society. It tells us that we must do some things and not do other things. It imposes penalties for breaking its laws and regulations.

In Plato's book, *The Republic*, he dreamed of a government by philosopher kings. In more recent times, the state has been seen as rightly resting on force. For some it is an end in itself. For others, the government was to assure them material prosperity, glorify their race, their religion, or their way of life.

In today's world, two extreme forms of government have emerged. The Marxists have a commitment to strong rule by the right people. Although the goal of the Marxist tradition is a time of peace and abundance for all, to date, Marxist-oriented states have been dictatorial in rule with a small elite group or a single individual exercising control.

There stands another tradition which is best exemplified in the recent history of Great Britain and in the United States and Canada. This view denies that there is such a thing as the right people who should hold a near-absolute sway over others. This tradition seeks to limit the powers of government and to create institutions and customs which make these limitations effective. This type of government is called a political democracy.

the latter form of government insists that no matter who comes to power, he or she will be (1) fallible in understanding, (2) limited in the capacity to be fair and equitable to all, (3) limited in capability to carry out his or her sense of understanding and sense of what is right, and (4) restricted by external forces to carry out whatever improvements for society he or she may undertake to follow.

Thus, they insist that governmental power should be split between different groups in the government itself. According to their definition of democracy, the majority should rule and power should be exercised through their representatives. This system of checks and balances, although relatively inefficient, provides for the expansion of human rights, liberties, and justice.

91

Questions:

1. Does majority rule ever happen in a nation?

2. If your answer to question #1 is "yes," then consider the following: Women represent almost 52% of the American people and are still considered to be a minority group. Why?

3. Who is more likely to serve time in prison: (1) a black male who steals $100 from a convenience store, or (2) a white male banker who embezzles ten thousand dollars over a period of a decade from the bank where he works? Research this one completely.

4. In our two cartoons, President Reagan is depicted as shirking his presidential responsibilities for the behaviors of his staff during 1985-1987. Study the hearings of the Iran-Contra Affair carefully. Write a position paper giving your opinion, based on your perception of the evidence presented, of the President's responsibility in this controversy.

Mind Builder
Selfish or Unselfish

The purpose of this exercise is to look at what values influence the difficult decisions people have to make.

1. Select seven or eight volunteers who are willing to pay 25¢ to take part in the experiment. If too few want to participate, tell the class that there is a chance to make money from the experiment.

2. Have the volunteers form a circle while the other members of the class observe. All quarters are collected before the experiment begins.

3. Place the money in the center of the circle and explain that in a given time limit the group must decide who gets all the money. Ten to fifteen minutes is a good time limit for the exercise.

4. All the money must go to one person. No deals to split the money after the game are permitted. No group leader is appointed.

5. There are two alternatives for the group in deciding who gets the money. First, no restrictions are placed on techniques, usually before very much time has elapsed the group will decide on luck as the means of distribution. Second, the group is instructed not to use luck as a means of distribution. This approach is the most effective.

(continued on the next page)

94

6. After a decision is made as to what student gets the money, the class discusses the experiment. By the way, the student keeps the money.
   — The class discusses the process by which the group reached a decision.
   — What values were demonstrated in making the decision?
   — Was the decision fair? Was it just?
   — Why did the group resort to luck if that approach was used?
   — Which members influenced the group decision the most? How was this done?
   — What does this tell us about leadership?

DILEMMA DEBATE #21:
FORCE IS ALL THEY UNDERSTAND

Let's reconsider many of the ideas that have been generated by these activities concerning *Peace on Earth*. Today, the United States is one of the more than 100 "sovereign" national states which comprise the international world community. Through its claim to sovereignty, each of these states declines to recognize any legal authority superior to its own. It does not feel bound to accept any decision arrived at without its consensus and reserves the right to oppose by force, if it so chooses, any attempt to impose such decisions upon it.

Many times, nations resolve their differences peacefully through negotiation, collective security, alliances, or arms limitation treaties. But sometimes an individual nation—even one which claims to promote peace and harmony—will resort to *force* in order to control other nations.

Mind Builder
Policy Makers/Decision Makers

Have students pay close attention to the situations where their wishes are overruled by someone who has more power, such as a teacher, parent, coach, etc. The student is to analyze five situations like this by:

1. Describing the situation.

2. Determining the type of authority.

3. Identifying the person's source of authority—how and why the person has power. Is the power legitimate? What makes it legitimate?

4. Cite one person who has power over this person.

96

Discussion

1. Study the cartoons associated with this activity.

2. Do you believe that a world community can be created from the attitude portrayed in the first cartoon? Give your reasons.

3. Answer the following questions:
   a. Do we as human beings have any rights which are morally superior to national rights?

   b. Could these rights be applied nationally and internationally to produce a better world? If so, how?

   c. If utter destruction is the only alternative to peace, what should our nation be doing to secure a permanent peace?

d. Although the United States is not at war with any other country, it is involved in wars around the globe. We assist other nations directly or indirectly with their own wars.

The cartoon, "Gave proof through the night..." illustrates this fact.

(i) Find out where and by what means the United States is now involved in other nations' wars.

(ii) Debate: "Should the United States be the guardian of world peace and freedom?"

...GAVE PROOF THROUGH THE NIGHT THAT OUR FLAG IS NOW THERE.

DILEMMA DEBATE #22:
THEN IT'S SETTLED

Most government officials are honest and desire to serve the public interest. Most of them give effective and efficient service and deserve more recognition than they receive. But, on occasion, even honest officials can easily fail to distinguish clearly between their private interests and the public interest. They sometimes get these two confused, assuming that their private interest is or ought to be the public interest also. Thus, they sometimes find it difficult to determine what morality in office really is.

Some people believe that standards of public morality have been steadily rising, even though they may not be improving as rapidly as the times demand. They comment that though there are occasional slumps or dips in the long-time trend, our standards in political life, at least at the national level, are higher today than at the beginning of this century and certainly much higher than in colonial days. We are slowly developing a concept of general welfare that gives us "a working pattern for public ethics," which says that "private profit by public servants, whether or not it is achieved at the expense of the public welfare, is corrupt."

A minority of governmental officials have carried on practices that have lowered the prestige of government and its officials. Anyone who scans the newspaper headlines of recent years will find accounts of these practices. They involve, among other things, tax scandals, voting frauds, political decisions influenced by gifts, protection of criminals, and shady business deals involving public agencies.

The two cartoons in this section depict the efforts of members of the National Security Council to get around the Bolen Amendment to a Treasury funding bill—in effect, to rewrite the law to suit their purposes. During the 1987 hearings, details of possibly illegal dealings with the Iranians and with the Central American Contras were elicited. Also, high profits made by some of the men involved were alleged. Because the law and the social order can never be a seamless garment of right, we must constantly judge our governmental system and alter it if alterations seem justified.

Activities:

1.   Read the following and summarize their findings in a written review:

"Past and Present Standards of Public Ethics in America: Are we improving?" *The Annals of the American Academy of Political and Social Science*, Vol. 280., pp. 1-8. Author: Estes Kefauver.   **99**

Ethical Standards in Government. A Report of a Subcommittee of the Senate Committee on Labor and Public Welfare. Washington, D.C.: U.S. Government Printing Office.

Code of Ethics for Government Service, House Document 103 of the 86th Congress. Washington, D.C.: U.S. Government Printing Office.

2. Based on your research into ethics and the government, is it your opinion that members of the NSC were involved in unethical and illegal practices? Give reasons for your answers.

3. One of the eight basic principles laid down by President John F. Kennedy as guidelines for his staff was, "No officer or employee of the Executive Branch shall use his office position for financial profit."

   Can you find instances where this ethical principle has been violated by members of the United States Government in recent years?

4. Finally, write your own code of ethics for members of the government. Present these to your class members and debate their merits. You may want to send the finished results to your representatives.

"NEVER MIND KUWAITI TANKERS— WE BETTER REFLAG OLLIE!"

Mind Builder
Rule Makers/Rule Breakers

Have the students:

1. Make a list of any current laws they would like to change.

2. Break into small groups and categorize these laws: Decide if they are in the best interest of:

    a. Society as a whole

    b. A particular community or societal segment

    c. A particular individual or special interest group.

3. On the chalkboard, total the conclusions of the entire class under these three headings.

Point: Rule-makers often become rule-breakers because of special interests.

" THEN IT'S SETTLED— GOVERNMENT OF THE COLONEL, BY THE COLONEL AND FOR THE COLONEL!... "

Mind Builder
Value Challenge

The purpose of this exercise is to encourage students to think seriously about the values that are the basis for their behavior.

Some Dominant Values:

Equality	Moral Orientation
Happiness	Progress
Freedom	Material Comfort
Work	Family
Achievement	Security
Salvation	Love

1. Have students select one of the values above that they have strong feelings about and prepare a two to three minute talk explaining the value and telling why it is important to them.

2. After listening to the talk, members of the class are to challenge or criticize the talk. They may question the validity of the argument, the validity of the value itself, the value of the value, and the right to hold the value.

3. After the exercise is completed, discuss the following questions:

    — What feelings were experienced in having your values challenged?

    — What type of challenge was the most threatening?

    — Did you want to change anything you said about your value?

    — Is your value held as strongly after having it challenged?

SELECTED READINGS

Baldwin, James, *Go Tell It on the Mountain*
Berger, Peter L., *The Noise of Solemn Assemblies*
Berger, Peter L., *The Precarious Vision*
Caldwell, Erskine, *Tobacco Road*
Crane, Stephen, *The Red Badge of Courage*
Denisoff, S.R., *Great Day Coming*
DuBois, W.E.B., *The Souls of Black Folk*
Einstein, Albert, *The World as I See It*
Erikson, K.T., *Everything in Its Path*
Faulkner, William, *The Sound and the Fury*
Frank, Anne, *Diary of a Young Girl*
Freeman, Jo (ed.), *Women: A Feminist Perspective*
Girvetz, Harry K., *Beyond Right and Wrong*
Glazer, Nathan, *American Judaism*
Goffman, Irving, *Encounters*
Golding, William, *Lord of the Flies*
Greeley, A.M., *Why Can't They Be Like Us?*
Hailey, Arthur, *In High Places*
Hardin, Garrett, *Exploring New Ethics for Survival/ The Voyage of The Spaceship Beagle*
Hawthorne, Nathaniel, *The Scarlet Letter*
Howard, John R., *The Cutting Edge*
Huxley, Aldous, *Brave New World*
Joseph, Alvin M., *Red Power*
Kemnitz, Thomas M. & Philip Fitch Vincent, *Computer Ethics*
Lee, Harper, *To Kill a Mockingbird*
Livingston, John A., *One Cosmic Instant*
Maya, Angelo, *I Know Why the Caged Bird Sings*
McGiffert, Michael, *The Character of Americans*
Melville, Herman, *Billy Budd*
Mills, C. Wright, *The Power Elite*
Moore, Wilbert E., *Economy, Society and Man*
More, Sir Thomas, *Utopia*
Orwell, George, *Animal Farm*
Orwell, George, *1984*
Packard, Vance, *The Hidden Persuaders*
Packard, Vance, *The Naked Society*
Packard, Vance, *The People Shapers*
Packard, Vance, *The Waste Makers*
Rawls, John, *A Theory of Justice*
Reich, Charles A., *The Greening of America*
Richter, Peyton E. (ed.), *Utopias*
Ross, Stephen David, *The Nature of Moral Responsibility*

103

Rossi, Alice K., *The Feminist Papers*
Ruggiero, Vincent Ryan, *The Moral Imperative*
Salinger, J.D., *The Catcher in the Rye*
Selekman, Benjamin M., *A Moral Philosophy for Management*
Shute, Nevil, *On the Beach*
Stowe, Harriet Beecher, *Uncle Tom's Cabin*
Swift, Jonathan, *Gulliver's Travels*
Toffler, Alvin, *Future Shock*
Toffler, Alvin, *The Third Wave*
Twain, Mark, *Life on the Mississippi*
Wells, H.G., *The Time Machine*
Wilson, John, *Thinking with Concepts*
Wilson, Sloan, *The Man in the Gray Flannel Suit*
Wright, Richard, *Blackboy*